bedtime
Butterfly Kisses

Dedicated to:

Braydon and Evelyn

Special Thanks to:

David Tansley

Ric and Sheryl Sawyer

Stephanie Lough-Camblin

Belinda the butterfly was bouncing on a breeze

She landed on my shoulder to give it a squeeze.

"How do you do?"
Belinda sang
so sweet.

"May I rest here
a moment while my
heart slows a beat?"

She stopped for a moment then began to explore
Travelling my arm from my neck toward the floor.

Three times she wandered from shoulder to finger
She was so sweet – I hoped she would linger.

Perched in my hand, she began stroking my palm
it tickled before I realized it made me feel calm.
She drew circles and hearts with her nose on my skin.

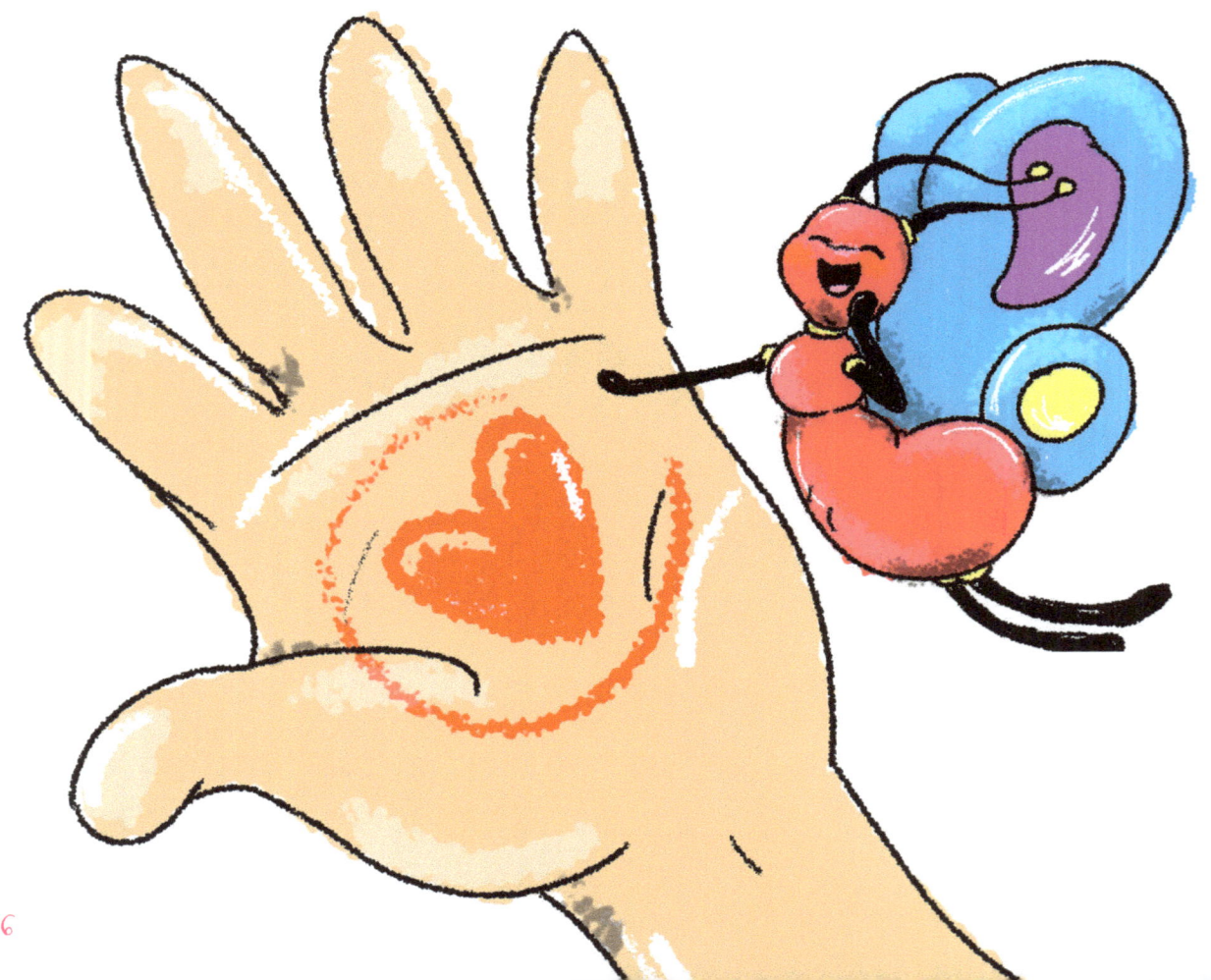

Then she giggled and climbed
right back up to my chin.

She fluttered a kiss to my cheek and rubbed my head

Gently she whispered, "Baby, time for bed."
My eyelids were heavy as I tried to protest
To forget Belinda when I woke I'd deeply regret!

Belinda's wings push the air across my sleepy face
Like bedtime kisses made out of the most delicate lace

"Rest well little one," She sings,
"And don't think about your sorrow.
If you go to sleep now I can come back tomorrow."

About the Author:

Jennifer Tansley is an artist, author and Registered Massage Therapist that lives with her family in Haldimand County Ontario.

Connect with her on Facebook and Instagram @riversidermt and @riversidecreativecottage

Bedtime Butterfly Kisses
Copyright © 2018 by Jennifer Sarah Tansley
Illustrator: Chrissy Schram

All rights reserved. No part of this publication may be reproduced, distributed, or transmitted in any form or by any means, including photocopying, recording, or other electronic or mechanical methods, without the prior written permission of the author, except in the case of brief quotations embodied in critical reviews and certain other non-commercial uses permitted by copyright law.

Tellwell Talent
www.tellwell.ca

ISBN
978-0-2288-0085-9 (Paperback)

www.ingramcontent.com/pod-product-compliance
Lightning Source LLC
LaVergne TN
LVHW072016060526
838200LV00059B/4686